FastTrack
MUSIC INSTRUCTION

Drums 2
Songbook 1

INTRODUCTION

Welcome back to FastTrack®!

Hope you enjoyed *Drums 2* and are ready to play some hits. Have you and your friends formed a band? Or do you feel like jamming with the CD? Either way, make sure you're relaxed and comfortable…it's time to play!

As always, don't try to bite off more than you can chew. If your arms are tired, take some time off. If you get frustrated, put down your sticks, sit back and just listen to the CD. If you forget a technique or rhythm, go back and learn it. If you're doing fine, think about finding an agent.

CONTENTS

ABOUT THE CD

Again, you get a CD with the book! Each song in the book is included on the CD, so you can hear how it sounds and play along when you're ready.

Each example on the CD is preceded by one measure of "clicks" to indicate the tempo and meter. Pan right to hear the drum part emphasized. Pan left to hear the accompaniment emphasized.

HAL•LEONARD®
CORPORATION

7777 W. BLUEMOUND RD. P.O. BOX 13819 MILWAUKEE, WI 53213

Visit Hal Leonard online at
www.HalLeonard.com

LEARN SOMETHING NEW EACH DAY

We know you're eager to play, but first we need to explain a few new things. We'll make it brief—only one page...

Melody and Lyrics

There's that extra musical staff again! Remember, this additional staff (on top) shows you the song's melody and lyrics. This way, you can follow along more easily as you play your accompaniment part, whether you're playing, resting or showing off with a solo . . . well, sometimes drummers do get a solo.

And if you happen to be playing with a singer, this new staff is their part.

Endings

In case you've forgotten some of the **ending symbols** from Songbook 1, here's a reminder:

1st and 2nd Endings

These are indicated by brackets and numbers:

Simply play the song through to the first ending, then repeat back to the first repeat sign, or beginning of the song (whichever is the case). Play through the song again, but skip the first ending and play the second ending.

D.S. al Coda

When you see these words, go back and repeat from this symbol: 𝄋

Play until you see the words "To Coda" then skip to the Coda, indicated by this symbol: 𝄌

Now just finish the song.

That's about it! Enjoy the music...

4-10

① Back in the U.S.S.R.

Words and Music by John Lennon and Paul McCartney

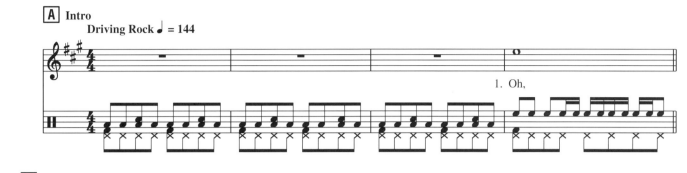

A Intro

Driving Rock ♩ = 144

1. Oh,

B Verse

flew in from Mi-a-mi Beach B. O. A. C. ___ Did-n't get to bed last night. ___ On
2. Been a-way so long I hard-ly know the place. ___ Gee, ___ it's good to be back home. ___ Leave

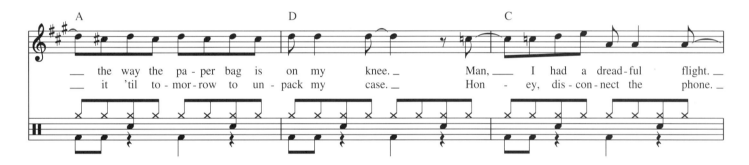

___ the way the pa-per bag is on my knee. ___ Man, ___ I had a dread-ful flight. ___
___ it 'til to-mor-row to un-pack my case. ___ Hon-ey, dis-con-nect the phone. ___

C Chorus

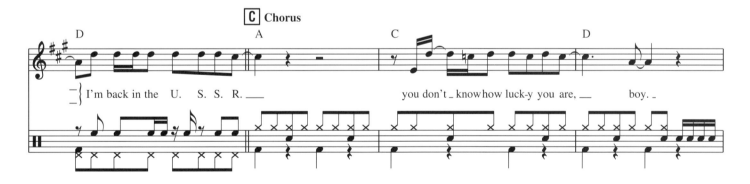

I'm back in the U. S. S. R. ___   you don't know how luck-y you are, ___ boy. ___

1.

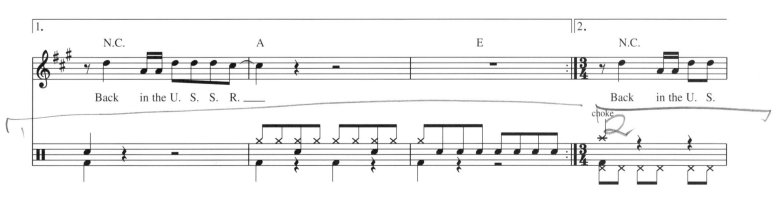

Back   in the U. S. S. R. ___

choke

2.

Back   in the U. S.

back in the U. S. back in the U. S. S. R. ____ Well, the

Bridge

D7   A7

U - krane girls real-ly knock me out. __ They leave the _ west be - hind. __ And

D   Db   C   B   E7   D7

Mos - cow girls make me sing and shout _ that Geog-ia's al-ways on my mi mi mi mi mi mi mi mi _ mind. __

To Coda ⊕

E **Guitar Solo**

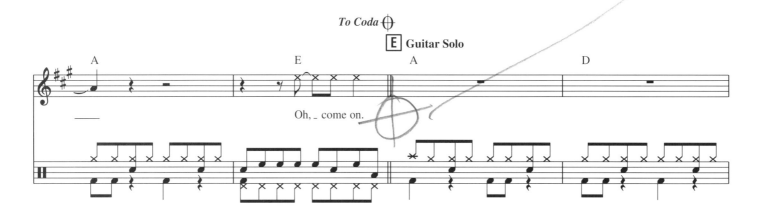

A   E   A   D

____   Oh, _ come on.

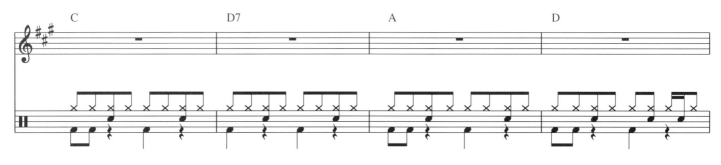

C   D7   A   D

F Chorus

Yeah _ I'm back in the U. S. S. R. _ You don't _ know how luck-y you are, _

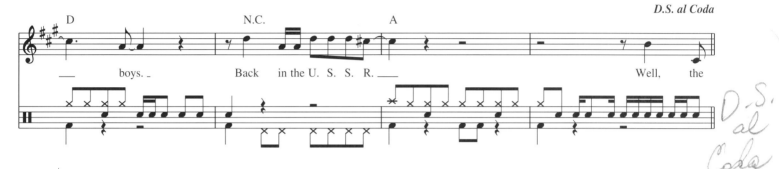

D.S. al Coda

_ boys. _ Back in the U. S. S. R. _ Well, the

Coda

G Verse

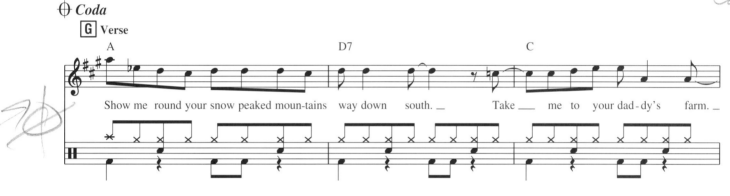

Show me round your snow peaked moun-tains way down south. _ Take _ me to your dad-dy's farm. _

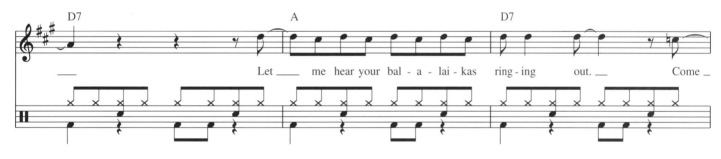

Let _ me hear your bal - a - lai - kas ring - ing out. _ Come _

H Outro-Chorus

_ and keep your com - rade _ warm. I'm back in the U. S. S. R. _

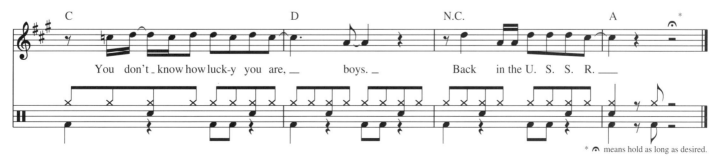

You don't _ know how luck-y you are, _ boys. _ Back in the U. S. S. R. _

* ⌒ means hold as long as desired.

5

Born to Be Wild

Words and Music by Mars Bonfire

3-25-10

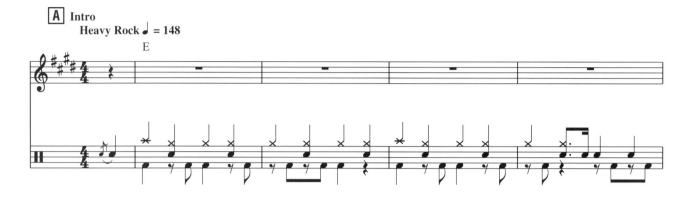

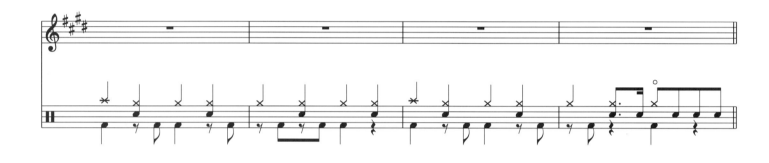

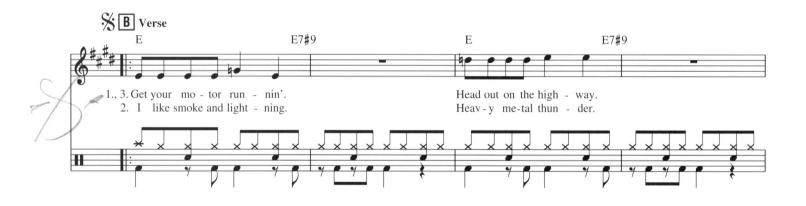

MCA Music Publishing

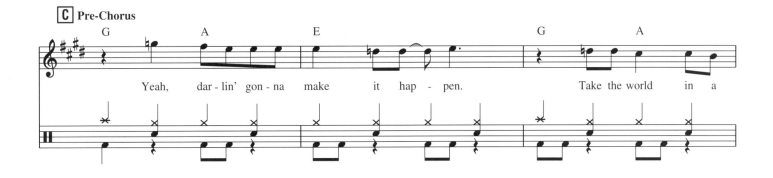

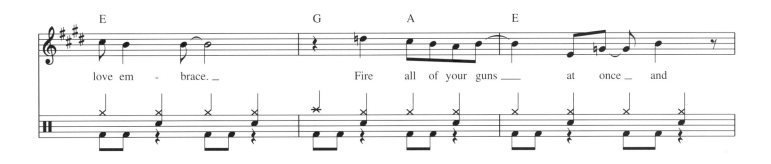

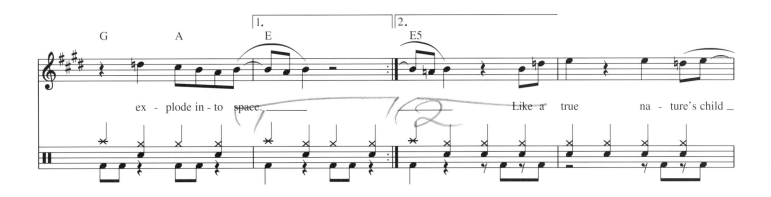

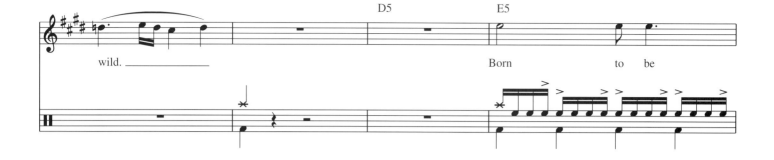

D5   E5

wild. _____

Born   to   be

To Coda ⊕

E   D5

wild. _____

E **Organ Solo**

E

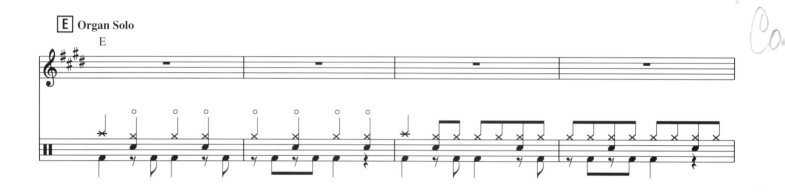

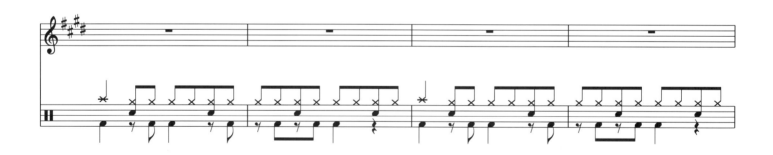

E7#9

Flams

D.S. al Coda
(take 2nd ending)

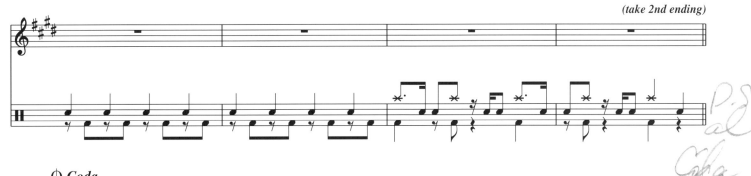

⊕ *Coda*

F Outro

E5

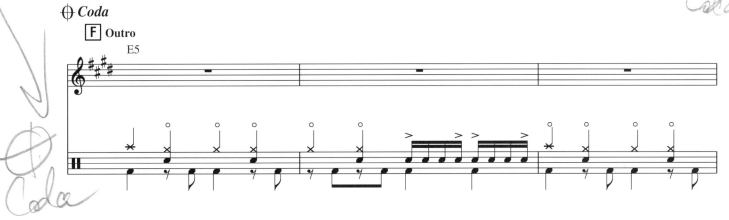

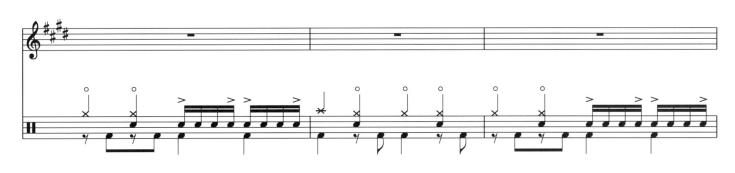

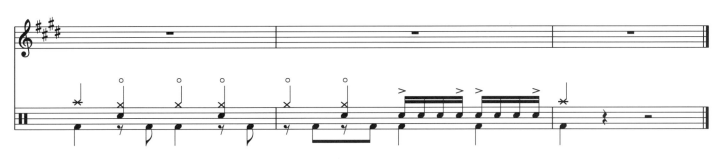

❸ I'm Your Hoochie Coochie Man

C Chorus

what this all a-bout. I'm here. ___
Hoo-chie Coo-chie man. I'm here. ___
don't you mess with me. I'm here. ___

Ev - 'ry-bod-y knows ___ I'm

here.

I'm the Hoo - chie Coo-chie man. ___

1., 2.

Ev - 'ry-bod-y knows ___ I'm here.

2. I

3.

Ev - 'ry-bod-y knows ___ I'm here.

Imagine

Words and Music by John Lennon

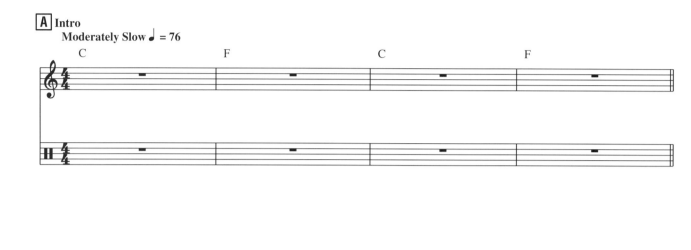

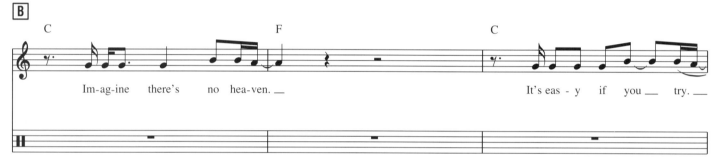

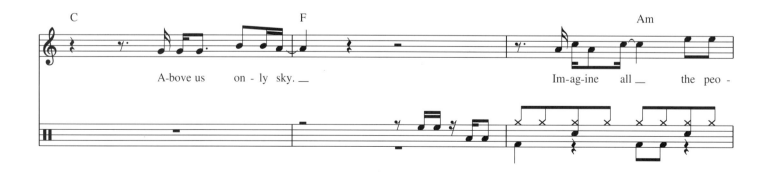

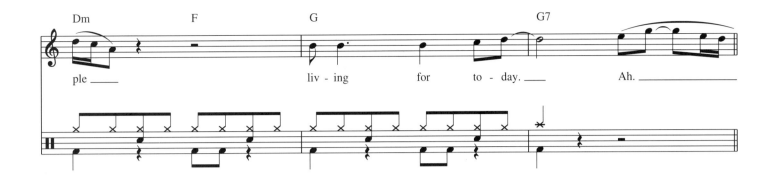

ple _____ liv - ing for to - day. _____ Ah. _____

C

Im-ag-ine there's no coun - tries. It is - n't hard _____ to do. _____
Im-ag-ine no pos - ses - sions. I won-der if _____ you can. _____

Noth-ing to kill _____ or die _____ for,
No need for greed _ or hun - ger,

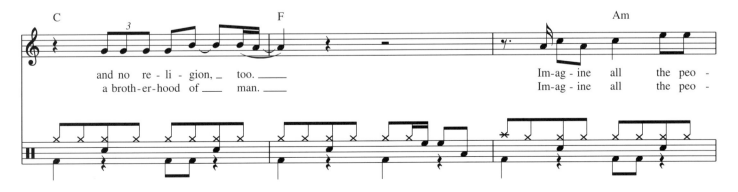

and no re - li - gion, _ too. _____ Im-ag - ine all the peo -
a broth-er-hood of _____ man. _____ Im-ag - ine all the peo -

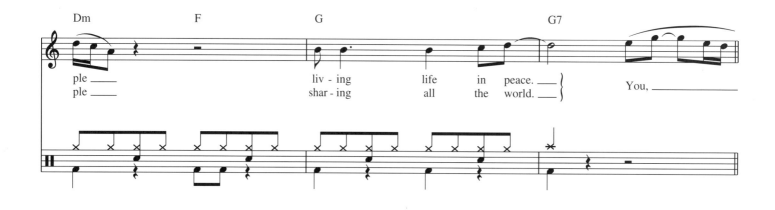

ple _____ liv - ing life in peace. _____ } You, _____
ple _____ shar - ing all the world. _____ }

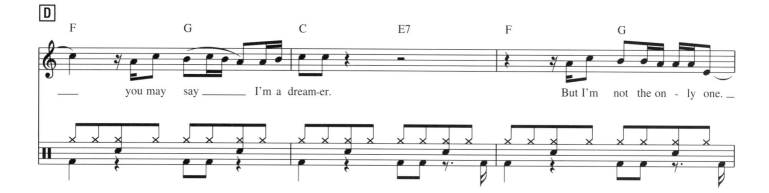

_____ you may say _____ I'm a dream-er. But I'm not the on - ly one. _____

_____ I hope some day _____ you'll join us _____

and the world _____ will be as one. _____ live as one. _____

got me on my knees, Lay-la. ____

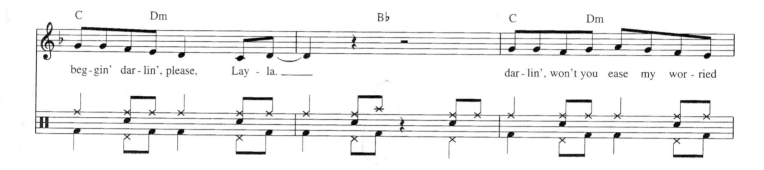

beg-gin' dar-lin', please, Lay-la. ____ dar-lin', won't you ease my wor-ried

D Outro - Chorus

mind? Lay - la, ____

Got me on my knees, Lay-la. ____ Beg-gin' dar-lin', please, Lay-la. ____

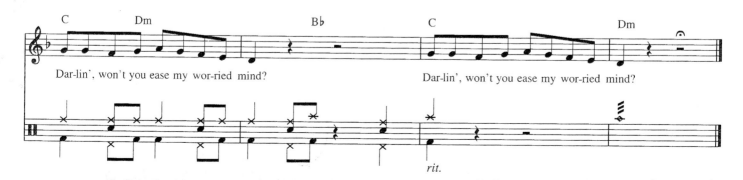

Dar-lin', won't you ease my wor-ried mind? Dar-lin', won't you ease my wor-ried mind?

rit.

⑤ Layla

Words and Music by Eric Clapton and Jim Gordon

B Chorus

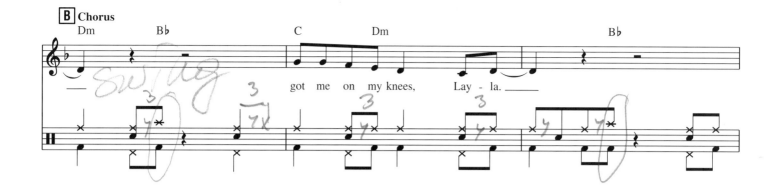

got me on my knees, Lay - la. _____

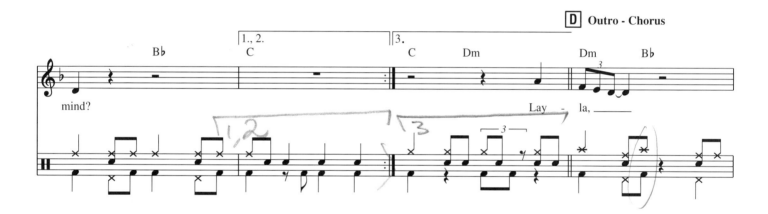

beg-gin' dar-lin', please, Lay - la. _____ dar-lin', won't you ease my wor-ried

D Outro - Chorus

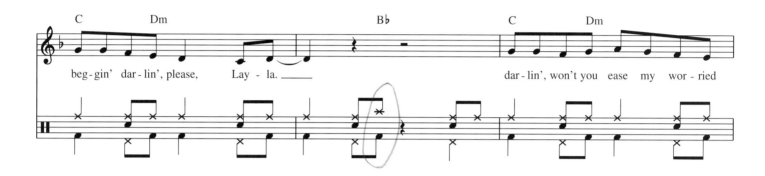

1., 2. 3.

mind? Lay - la, _____

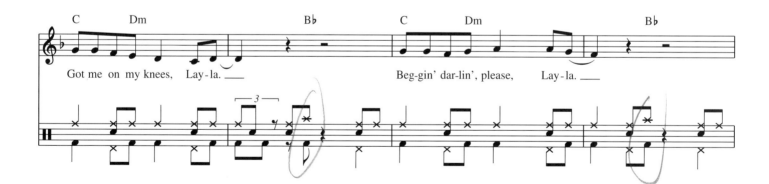

Got me on my knees, Lay - la. _____ Beg-gin' dar-lin', please, Lay - la. _____

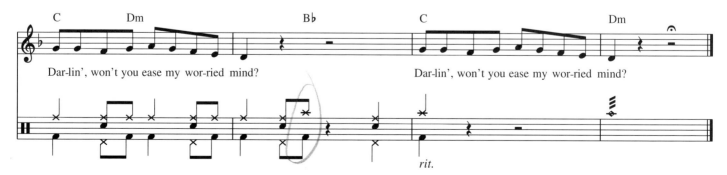

Dar-lin', won't you ease my wor-ried mind? Dar-lin', won't you ease my wor-ried mind?

rit.

2-11-10

6 Maggie May

Words and Music by Rod Stewart and Martin Quittenton

tried _ an - y - more. _____ You led me a - way from
tried _ an - y - more. _____ You led me a - way from
tried _ an - y - more. _____ You led me a - way from
nev - er seen your face. _____ You made a first class fool out - a

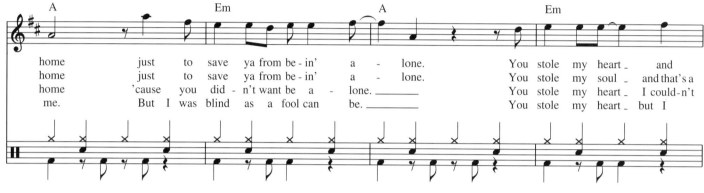

home just to save ya from be - in' a - lone. You stole my heart _ and
home just to save ya from be - in' a - lone. You stole my soul _ and that's a
home 'cause you did - n't want be a - lone. _____ You stole my heart _ I could-n't
me. But I was blind as a fool can be. _____ You stole my heart _ but I

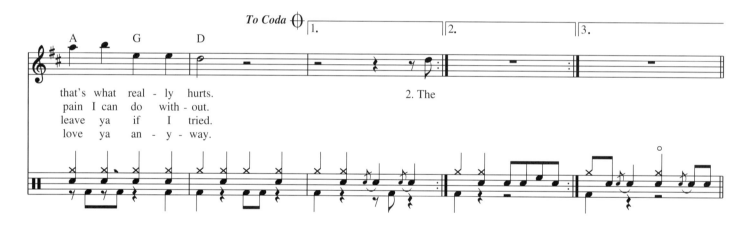

that's what real - ly hurts.
pain I can do with - out.   2. The
leave ya if I tried.
love ya an - y - way.

D Guitar Solo

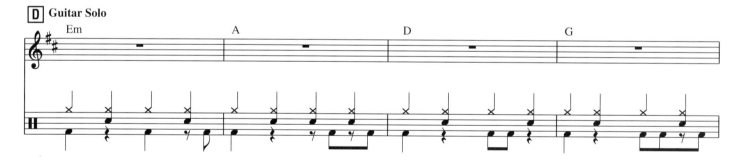

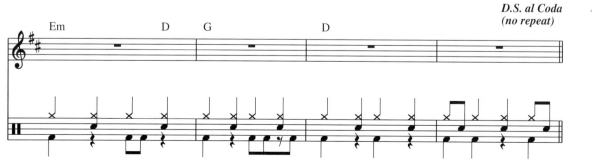

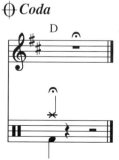

7 No Particular Place to Go

Words and Music by Chuck Berry

C Guitar Solo

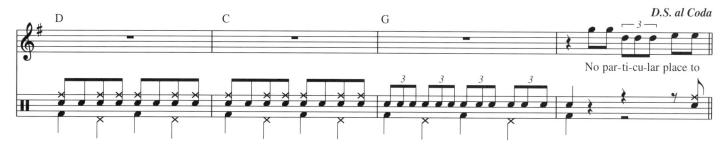

D.S. al Coda

No par-ti-cu-lar place to

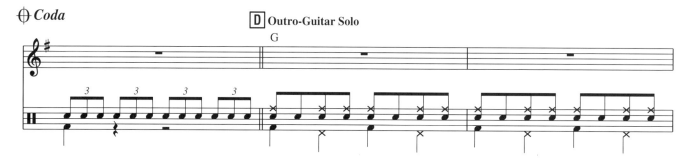

⊕ *Coda*   D Outro-Guitar Solo

1-25-10

⑧ Takin' Care of Business

Words and Music by Randy Bachman

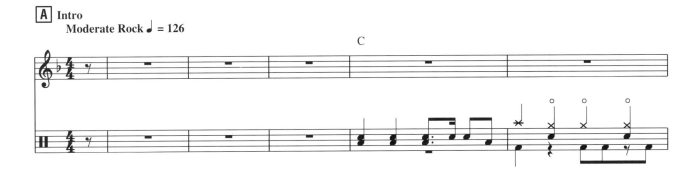

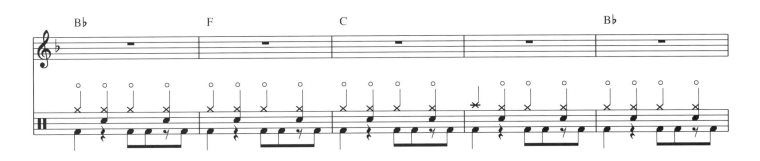

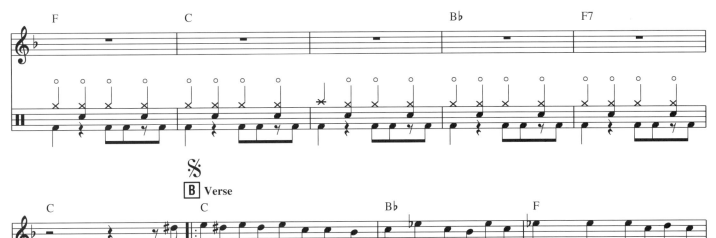

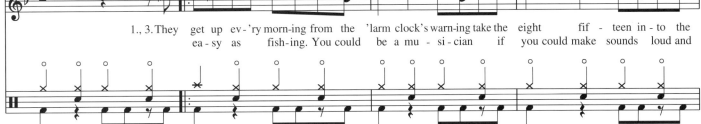

1., 3. They get up ev-'ry morn-ing from the 'larm clock's warn-ing take the eight fif - teen in - to the
ea - sy as fish-ing. You could be a mu - si - cian if you could make sounds loud and

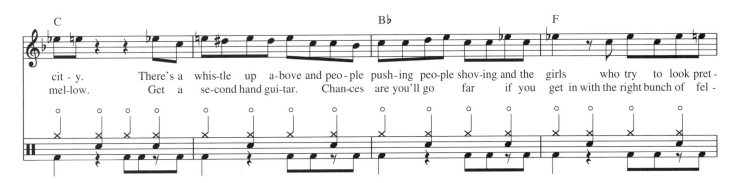

cit - y. There's a whis-tle up a-bove and peo - ple push-ing peo-ple shov-ing and the girls who try to look pret -
mel-low. Get a se-cond hand gui-tar. Chan-ces are you'll go far if you get in with the right bunch of fel -

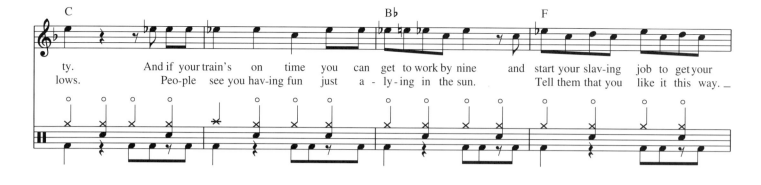

ty.   And if your train's on time you can get to work by nine   and start your slav-ing job to get your
lows.   Peo-ple see you hav-ing fun just a - ly-ing in the sun.   Tell them that you like it this way. __

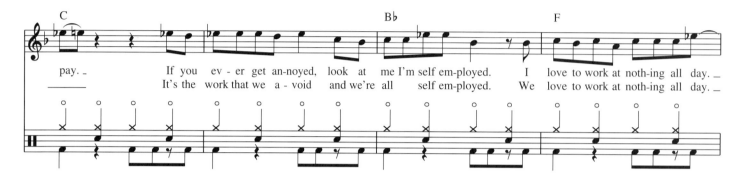

pay. __   If you ev - er get an-noyed, look at me I'm self em-ployed.   I love to work at noth-ing all day. __
_____   It's the work that we a - void and we're all self em-ployed.   We love to work at noth-ing all day. __

C Chorus

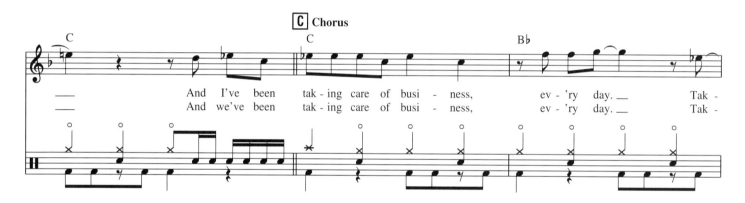

_____   And I've been tak - ing care of busi - ness, ev - 'ry day. __ Tak -
_____   And we've been tak - ing care of busi - ness, ev - 'ry day. __ Tak -

- ing care of busi - ness, ev - 'ry way. I've been tak - ing care of busi - ness, it's all mine. __ Tak -
- ing care of busi - ness, ev - 'ry way. I've been tak - ing care of busi - ness, it's all mine. __ Tak -

1.

To Coda ⊕

D Interlude

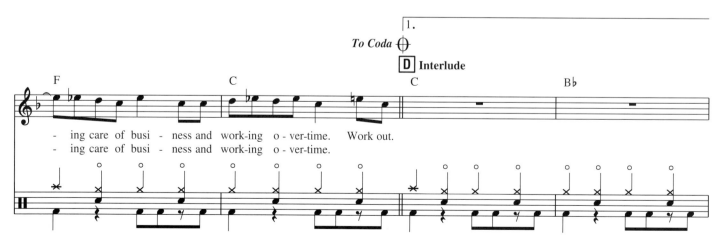

- ing care of busi - ness and work-ing o - ver-time. Work out.
- ing care of busi - ness and work-ing o - ver-time.

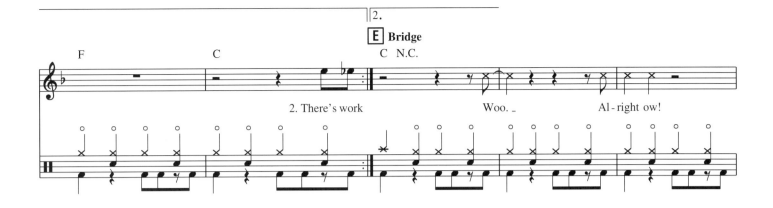

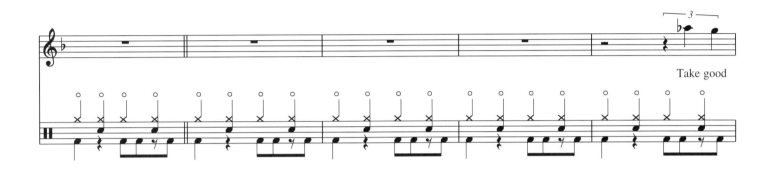

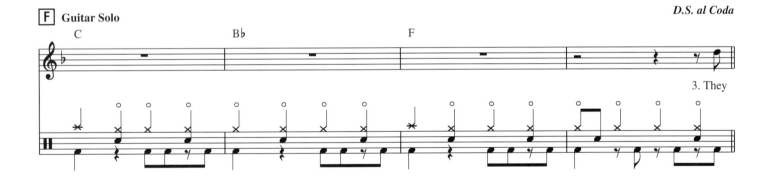

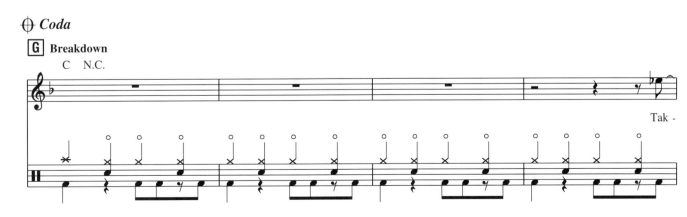

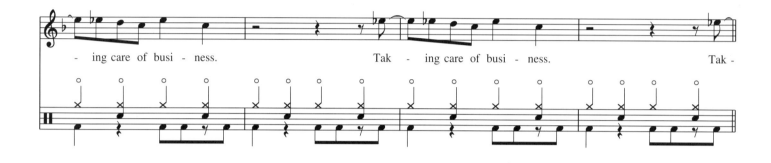

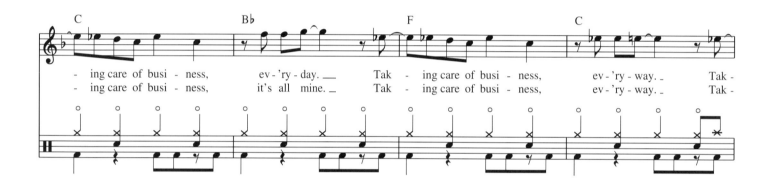

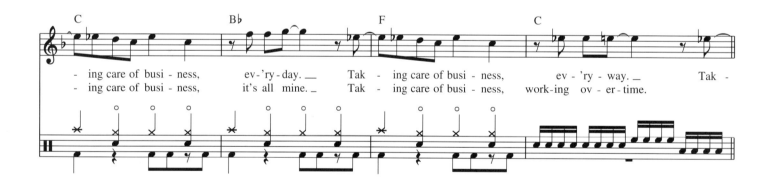

H **Outro-Chorus**

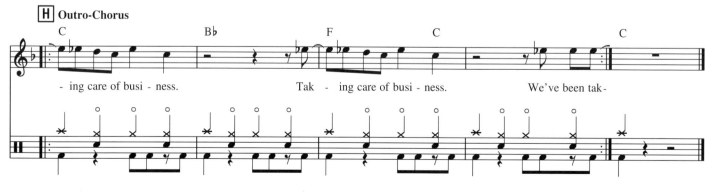